SOME DANCE

THE HUGH MACLENNAN POETRY SERIES

Editors: Allan Hepburn and Tracy Ware

TITLES IN THE SERIES

Waterglass   Jeffery Donaldson
All the God-Sized Fruit   Shawna Lemay
Chess Pieces   David Solway
Giving My Body to Science   Rachel Rose
The Asparagus Feast   S.P. Zitner
The Thin Smoke of the Heart   Tim Bowling
What Really Matters   Thomas O'Grady
A Dream of Sulphur   Aurian Haller
Credo   Carmine Starnino
Her Festival Clothes   Mavis Jones
The Afterlife of Trees   Brian Bartlett
Before We Had Words   S.P. Zitner
Bamboo Church   Ricardo Sternberg
Franklin's Passage   David Solway
The Ishtar Gate   Diana Brebner
Hurt Thyself   Andrew Steinmetz
The Silver Palace Restaurant   Mark Abley
Wet Apples, White Blood   Naomi Guttman
Palilalia   Jeffery Donaldson
Mosaic Orpheus   Peter Dale Scott
Cast from Bells   Suzanne Hancock
Blindfold   John Mikhail Asfour
Particles   Michael Penny
A Lovely Gutting   Robin Durnford
The Little Yellow House   Heather Simeney MacLeod
Wavelengths of Your Song   Eleonore Schönmaier
But for Now   Gordon Johnston
Some Dance   Ricardo Sternberg

Some Dance

Ricardo Sternberg

McGill-Queen's University Press
Montreal & Kingston • London • Ithaca

© Ricardo Sternberg 2014
ISBN 978-0-7735-4347-8 (paper)
ISBN 978-0-7735-9175-2 (ePDF)
ISBN 978-0-7735-9176-9 (ePUB)

Legal deposit first quarter 2014
Bibliothèque nationale du Québec

Printed in Canada on acid-free paper that is 100%
ancient forest free (100% post-consumer recycled),
processed chlorine free

McGill-Queen's University Press acknowledges the support
of the Canada Council for the Arts for our publishing
program. We also acknowledge the financial support
of the Government of Canada through the Canada Book
Fund for our publishing activities.

Library and Archives Canada Cataloguing in Publication

Sternberg, Ricardo, 1948–, author
Some dance / Ricardo Sternberg.

(Hugh MacLennan poetry series)
Poems.
Issued in print and electronic formats.
ISBN 978-0-7735-4347-8 (pbk.). –
ISBN 978-0-7735-9175-2 (ePDF). –
ISBN 978-0-7735-9176-9 (ePUB)

I. Title. II. Series: Hugh MacLennan poetry series

PS8587.T4711S66 2014   C811'.54   C2013-907087-7
                                    C2013-907088-5

This book was typeset by Interscript in 9.5/13 New Baskerville.

For Chrissy, her moxie

CONTENTS

I

An Invocation of Sorts   3
The Bench   4
New Canaan   5
As Patient of Doctor Ramon   9
A Note   12
Pairings   14
The Soaps   16
Such Wisdom   19
California Fado   20
The Island   21
The Exquisite Art   23
The Prodigal   24
Stories Need Never End though Most Do   26
The Bench   27

II

Across the Mystic River   31
Orpheus   33
Echo   35
At It   36
Blues   37
Meal   38
Dip   39
The Green Bird   40

No Love Lost 42

Beginning with Isaiah 45

The Reckoning 47

The Almighty 49

In the Metro 51

Back and Forth 53

The Bees 54

Ars Longa, Vita Brevis 55

Fishing 58

Morals 60

Obit 61

Skills 63

The Good Brazilian 64

The Word 66

First One Thing and Then Another 68

A Prince's Soliloquy 70

Biography 72

Berkeley Is in Brazil 73

Kings 75

Manual 77

Some Dance 79

Acknowledgments 81

I

AN INVOCATION OF SORTS

Niceties dispensed, muse,
give it to me straight,
intravenous, undiluted, right
into this arm I write with.

Here or hereabouts
(I'm never quite sure)
a show of modesty
is expected so I admit

the gift is not commensurate
to the task at hand:
such a small wingspan,
my fear of heights.

So silver my drab tongue.
But as for theme: leave it to me
to come up with something
that while not highfalutin,

carries a whiff of the sublime.
Finally, don't just hang around
after giving me my dose. Look:
I'm really, really grateful. Now *adios*.

THE BENCH

Forget the fiddle faddle,
make do with just one fact:
blueness runs deep as this ocean
he stares at from the bench
here where the bay narrows
to a stone throat words rush through
gushing at full throttle
as if with too much to say
and hardly the breath to say it
while he, scrambling events from his life
with fiction and the TV soaps,
nudges the scales in his favour
but getting no purchase on truth
has almost convinced himself
that, throughout,
he merely did what needed done.

NEW CANAAN

I

A hummer, a whistler, a man
bent on keeping the blues at bay,
at the slightest peep from sorrow
he turns tail and runs away
lacking perhaps some enzyme
to properly process grief
as the mere hint of discord
throws him into such a funk
his passports are at the ready
as are contingency plans
should he find himself again,
unravelled and unsteady,
but shouldn't he know by now
that as fast as he might go
trouble hitches a ride in his pocket
and to prove it he might remember this:

II

The universe practically hummed
when they met and she said
we're standing smack on the fault
and my name is, guess what, Andréa
and this meeting has been foretold
to this very hour and day
three weeks ago by my astrologist
who dropped acid and his MBA
to train in an ashram in India
and was, you know, into stars,
for Venus was ascending
and Saturn transiting through
my second house, the house of wealth,
but she took wealth to mean just love
and that a van would be leaving soon
so, here, take a long puff on this,
and tomorrow, under a new moon,
they could both be in New Canaan
and would he like to come along
and he said he would and he did.

III

Everyone a vegetarian,
coffee strictly *verboten,*
the commune was not for him
and though he liked the sex
he cared little for the hours,
waking up with the roosters
to meditate on an empty stomach
while bad breath and night odours
proved to be impediments
to the aimed-for transcendence
insisting, as they did, the body
holds the spirit in a hammer lock
and his the worst of all
for as they sat down to their gruel
his loquacious stomach growled
in such long, drawn-out sentences
he took to calling it Cicero
and when sent into town for feed
he was caught at the local Wendy's
and the camel's back was broken
for Brother Bill hauled him in,
asked him to leave and he did
with no time to say goodbye, Andréa.

IV

Unjust, this caricature of Andréa
drawn some forty years to the day
since they met at the fault line
for, in fact, he soon recognized
she had qualities he sorely lacked
such as, for instance, a backbone,
he who drifted like a jellyfish
and though she never accused
he sensed the disappointment
when she tracked him down
five or six years after Canaan
to find him stalled but revving,
running errands across the border
for the sleazebag, Doctor Ramon,
while she, after leaving the commune
finished a nursing degree
and made ready to ship out
to work in a village in Africa
from whence she would not return.

AS PATIENT OF DOCTOR RAMON

I

When, uninsured, he drove to Mexico,
this optimist could not have guessed
that such a simple operation
(demoted to a "procedure")
could quickly take a turn for the worse
and only when he saw himself
(as if by an eye hovering above)
under the green, latexed hands
of a woozy Doctor Ramon,
did he finally realize that yes
he was this close to giving up the ghost
when a tunnel cracked open and a voice
told him to move towards the light
while a chorus of nurses intoned:
and he so young, so young and intestate

II

He'd been wheeled from Emerge
to a bright operating room
where Ramon, though scrubbed,
arrived at the theatre besotted,
under the influence of drugs
too numerous to count
for that very morning he'd found
the pillow next to his vacant
and when, in search of answers,
he entered the bathroom there it was,
the message left by Mercedes
using lipstick in lieu of a crayon,
a garish scrawl that simply said
  Basta! cabron!
and try as he might to remember
where their romance could have derailed
he could think of nothing except ...

 well here is the thought repressed:
the oh-so-innocent words
whispered *en passant* to Claudine
had been overheard by Mercedes
and been seriously misunderstood.

III

It was I, bragged the nurse
outside the hospital chapel,
who rescued that gringo
when Ramon dropped the scalpel
and in less time than it takes
to say "Maria Inês Miraflores"
had him properly sutured.
(To think blind prejudice
kept me out of medical school!)
That final knot I tied
with a quick flamenco flourish,
then bent down to kiss
the gringuito's sedated eyes
wondering what unhinged the doctor
just yesterday, hunky-dory,
today, coming apart at the seams.

A NOTE

Hey Sugar! Remember me?
read the note he found
those many years later
among the broken pencils,
old glasses and keys
as he cleared the apartment
making ready to leave
and though the acid of time
had bleached the card
the events recalled
in pink arabesque
seemed vaguely familiar
but surely someone else
had lived them for today,
standing by the window,
staring at his frozen yard,
he doubted he'd ever been
that tropical swain
who, done with dancing,
danced her out the door,
then took her to the grove
of palm trees in the dunes
where, as the note recalled,
"under the moon our bliss
has been etched in silver"
and just as he began

to consider that perhaps
– if this was not a movie –
all this happened and yes
indeed happened to him,
he recalled this billet-doux
he had filched years ago
when Ramon turned his back
to seal up the contraband box
he would drive across the border
dressed, this time, as a priest.

While a pair of Canada geese
peck at grass beneath his bench,
he faces Monterey Bay and lets
his mind meander then settle
on Noah: how, when the time came,
those pairs entered the oil-lit ark
still fragrant with the resin
of freshly hewn wood
then settled as the skies grew dark.

Next he thinks of Flaubert's Emma:
after months of dilly-dallying
(the walks, the sighs, the long, long looks,
their eyes so full of serious speech
was how Flaubert described it)
she is alone with young Leon
unlacing her boots as the carriage
rattles through cobblestones streets
and, in its shuttered dark,
she moves away from her marriage,
giving herself, deliciously, to sweet Leon.

Then, a lifetime or so ago,
how they themselves
leaving a highrise party
entered the lift in a fever
to hear Sly of the Family Stone
sing he could take them higher
but stopped the car between floors
to have a go at it, oblivious
to a buzzer that rang and rang,
and threats to call the police.

When the lift finally landed
they stepped into the lobby,
bowed deeply to the concierge,
then waltzed out hand in hand.
But just now, out on the bay
a sea lion barks to its mate
and he's left with this:
o what a torture it is to remember
his nimble fingers, her firm flesh.

THE SOAPS

I

The gravity of his situation
demanded a nimble response,
some rhetorical sleight-of-hand,
dexterous verbiage, the gift of gab
that would at once persuade her
and reverse the impending disaster
when she, made suddenly aware
of attenuating circumstances,
would drop the knife with a clatter
or so he imagined and further,
prone as he was to optimism,
could almost taste Victoria's tears,
the balm of forgiveness flowing,
as they sign a mid-afternoon truce
on the sheets of the king-size bed.

II

Never mind the suspense:
he was not up to the task,
the fact self evident when he spoke,
gimping out of the starting gate
advancing such a meandering defense,
one so full of obfuscation and fog
you wondered whether done on purpose
out of some harebrained, half-baked strategy
or simply in ignorance of her dark mood,
her silence having played out enough rope
for him to hang himself and when
– poor lamb, self driven to slaughter –
he slipped in a sly reference
to "The Post-Modern Duties of the Wife"
why, she renewed her grip on the knife,
her green eyes opened wide
and she began to walk towards him.

III

It was her mother, Miranda,
who brought back his clothes
stuffed in a garbage bag
dropped by his front door.
She spat on his welcome mat,
scribbled obscenities on his mail
then took off, gunning the Jag.
His linen suits, his silk ties,
his tailored shirts of Egyptian cotton
but he did not have to look
to surmise that his watches,
his gold cufflinks or mother
of pearl tie-clip were lost,
kept to be passed on as gifts
to the very next *hombre*
to homestead her bedroom.
By then he was resigned
and felt lucky that knife
had merely kissed his cheek
then slashed through empty air.

SUCH WISDOM

Herodotus thought the Persians wise
for the care they took with each decision:
asking the question sober at first
then drunk, asking it again
and if the answers tallied
no doubt was left as to their merit
and implementation quickly followed.
So as soon as he left the hospital
self-conscious of his bandaged cheek,
in the cave-like darkness of the Ali Baba
with its garish, neon minaret
he asked the question: should I go?
and, sober, quickly answered yes
then drunk much later asked again
and, slurred out a slower yes
slipping off the bar stool to the floor
where he promptly fell asleep
until morning came and he went
moving west and changing coasts
billeting first in his brother's house
and, once thrown out, in this condo
he could ill afford but could not pass up.

CALIFORNIA FADO

Time passes and heals all wounds
then passes some more and scars
are effaced, the memory gone
of disasters that brought him here.

So as he sits on the deck and surveys
the foam-fringed curve of the bay,
the very air seems saturated
with light, a golden pollen of promise

inducing a lotus torpor, a letting go
in the most curmudgeonly of spirits,
never mind this man, inveterate optimist,

who believes ha ha his ship's sailed into port
when flying in fast below radar
fate or its proxy is making a move.

THE ISLAND

Little more, it appears
when he lifts his eyes
after dream-waves drop him
ragged, rock-battered,
salt-stung on the beach
than the cartoon island
with its single palm tree
under which, exhausted,
shipwrecked, a sailor lies.

But a few days later
walking on the lee side
he finds a cave, a stream,
a patch of berries, the gold
of honey-combs treasured
in the dark of a tree.

A herd of goats finds him,
follow him everywhere.
Bearded apostles, they nibble
at his hair, chew his laces
and, one night while he sleeps,
eat his one and only book
leaving behind a torn page
where gold-leafed, a wooden god
stands in a melon patch
and can protect nothing.

The years flash by.
By flicker of fire light
he reads that half page
at first distractedly
then, sensing meaning
moves below the surface,
slowly blowing breath
into each syllable.

Now he braids his beard
and walks bitter beneath
a nimbus of white hair.

When sirens awake him,
he returns in mid-question:
what is man, he is asking,
if not that crop left untended
under the blind eyes
of the scarecrow god?

THE EXQUISITE ART

Better to marry than to burn
– St. Paul to the Corinthians –
thus granting a wee advantage
to the holy vows of matrimony
and though this one will confess
he had both married *and* burned,
Cynthia comes to him today
in the coolness of this ocean breeze
as she was at the final decree
when the flourish of signatures
freed them from the fever
that had made them masters
of that most exquisite art:
how else describe the deftness
with which they went at each other
through their humdrum hell,
until combustion consumed its fuel
leaving them perplexed, spent,
then close though wary pals.

THE PRODIGAL

Aren't you the one
who waved goodbye
then left for thirty years
only to return today
expecting us all to say:
stranger, good to see you.
Sit down, tell us your stories,
hear a few of our own.

While you were away
life moved as it does,
its engine never stops:
disasters following always
the heels of celebrations.
Crops we plant, thrive
and are then harvested
or, plagued by drought
are not worth the effort
and are ploughed back
into the ground. The same
for so many of us.
Notice we move carefully,
knowing the heart holds
a hidden trap door
and remembering friends
who now sail underground.

Dropped in the plush of satin,
steering baronial caskets,
they try to cross the river
believing that in so doing
they'll erase all traces of memory.

Upstairs, the rest of us
do work that must be done:
so much of it just plain forgetting,
letting go of those sad sailors,
waiting our prodigal's return
for the chance to say:
Stranger, good to see you.
Sit down, tell us some stories.
Here are few of our own.

STORIES NEED NEVER END
THOUGH MOST DO

Think of Odysseus, that tricky man,
the way the gods played him
for twenty years then dropped him
asleep in Ithaca, so discombobulated
he could not recognize upon waking
his own kingdom and began to wonder
what further troubles would the gods inflict
if they wished to delay a while longer
that moment he had yearned for
since turning his back on the rubble
the boys had made of Troy:
to be gathered in the arms of sweet Penelope.
Clumsy as that Greek was wily,
this man, nodding by the shore
who thinks that he has suffered,
has not suffered nearly enough
nor been tempered by his sufferings
into something better than what he was.

THE BENCH

The sea moves its blue shuttle
coming to shore, then receding,
then coming again and each time
it recedes it hoards away more light
as it weaves this winter evening
when he decided to come down
and take the show slowly in:
the egrets, the buffle heads,
the snowy plover, the pelicans
and perhaps, because of the chill,
no one is there to see him slump
light-headed, light-hearted, wondering
what ever would happen to that boy
standing across the dark waters
feeding out line to the small kite
that stutters in the wind then rises
as the sun finally sinks
and the roads of the world grow dark.

II

ACROSS THE MYSTIC RIVER

The Mystic River runs from the Mystic Lakes to the Boston Bay.

He had crossed the Mystic River,
so no wonder he felt unsure
as to whether he was (at last!)
seeing things as they truly were
or was (yet again?) bamboozled
Unable to decide, he thought
to consult Madame Florinda
who took his upturned hand in hers
and for a long time simply stared:

With a life line made of zigzags
I'd stay away from long term plans.
This line here, the ring of Venus,
breaks the free flow of energy
pointing to weakness and to stress.
But look: yours breaks before
it reaches Apollo's finger.
Hard to say what to make of it.
Your heart line is just a mess.

All of this so disconcerting
and as guidance simply useless.
Should he consult the I Ching?
No doubt his yin and yang
could be read as mere confusion,
if not opposites in graceful dance.

What he needed was a memorandum
of understanding between himself
and the world with all its things;
he needed that proverbial place
to stand on asked by Arquimedes,
not to move the world but to,
minimally, come to know it
as something other than himself.
To be able to pry apart:
this is object, this is subject
even though (confusion begins!)
he can be both. Difficult then
to stand at the mirror and reflect:
I am this. This is what I am.

ORPHEUS

Don't blame Orpheus
for that oblique
over-the-shoulder peek
taken to ensure
she was right behind.

Though he told himself
the way out is steep
she could have tripped,
her heel, still bruised
from that snake bite,

constantly to doubt,
to seek assurances,
the manic drive to do so
minute by minute
is some lover's curse.

The need to see her
at that very instant
was as exigent
as oxygen
for his next breath.

The light of our world
already visible to him,
far from his thoughts was
the intransigence of gods
or how long forever would take.

ECHO

It begins with her seeing birds:
some robins on a bird-bath
that stands in the backyard
halfway to the cedar fence.

In her kitchen, at the sink,
she is finishing dinner dishes
and, seeing birds splash with
nimble abandon, she becomes

entranced by a fragment
    (or is it a figment?) of memory:
who (and where?) had asked
"you coming in or what?"

"Or what" travels over the water,
ricochets off canyon walls and …
Kelsey. The Grand Canyon,
Easter weekend, 1968, as they

roamed through the national
parks but the memory dims now as
one of her children at her side asks,
enraged, for he had sensed her gone,

"Mother, were you listening at all?"

Intricately devious
this man
who blindsides,
hoodwinks even himself.

Just as he declares
that for now and forever
he's done with it,
there'd be no turning back,

he'd already backtracked
and by a circuitous route
returned to the spring
driven by the very thirst

he swore he'd quenched.

BLUES

Toot me something on your golden horn
he said to the musician.
I feel cold as my soul turns blue.

Jerry-build me an intricate song
full of those diminished sevenths
and enough thrust to push me through

bar by smoky bar, into oblivion.
Extricate me from thorny feelings,
put brain and heart to sleep.

Bring out a flute and its Bolivian
so sorrow can be trumped by sorrow.
Afford me, at any price, some peace.

Today I am bedeviled
befogged by this predicament:
will I find myself myself again tomorrow?

MEAL

Asked to eat crow
he did so and with such vengeance
he plucked the bird still warm
and from the collected feathers
made her a little pillow of nightmares.

Sweetmeats he set aside
to braise later in gingered port:
amuse-bouche for another time.
He rubbed the carcass
in a film of olive oil and lime.

He nailed the handful of cloves
to his own chest in a pattern
that spelled her secret name
then tucked the bird in a bed
of prunes and apricots,
flooded the pan with Madeira.

Later, contrite at the table
the white flag of surrender
in the flourish of his napkin,
slowly and deliberately
he ate the crow.

DIP

Once in a blue moon
she did and when she did
she startled moon and stars
with the brief flash
as, streaking meteor,
she plunged into the pond.

Shocked out of deep sleep
the pike turned to see
a blond ingot part
the waters with a hiss.

At once those frogs
were at a loss and silenced.
What could they say?
What song would ever
do justice to such event?

She swam about the dark,
a lazy golden thread
sewing up the pond
then stepped out, a brash
glistening, and dried her hair.

THE GREEN BIRD

The green bird nestled
in her voice,
sang from the dark wood
of her throat,

though he, as if grown deaf,
was no longer mesmerized
and could simply walk away.
The acrimonious tone

underlying her laments,
the eagerness
when she demanded kisses
(opening her blouse,

offering him her breasts)
imparted to his character,
lighthearted by nature,
a severity of demeanour

which, to his delight,
certain women found attractive.
At the mirror he rehearsed
a new syntax of gestures,

engineered distances
even she could not traverse.
Her crystal ball fumed,
predicting in its vapors

misfortunes and mishaps,
night sweats and tremors,
veiled threats from the police.
The deck of cards she dealt

confirmed the prognosis:
he be dead in every suit.
Sometimes he can forget
that crazy woman,

the ruckus she raised,
the hell she put him through.
Sometimes she returns
as she does today

as someone he knew once,
vaguely remembered now,
naked, save for the beadwork,
that green lilt around her throat.

Unable to string words tonight
In any manner that might please
he browses the mother lode
(what others call the *OED*)

by chance, Volume L through M,
and is immediately convinced
of the need to bring back
(banned to dial. vulgar and arch.)

the useful La! – exclamation
formerly used to introduce
or accompany a conventional phrase,
address, or to call attention

to an emphatic statement.
As in: He'd a caressing way
but la! You know it's a
manner natural to poets.

Poets, when unable to write
(a condition known as blocked)
often drink, make bad companions
and should they drink excessively,

quickly reach labescency
(tottering state or condition).
They awake a loggerhead
(a thick-headed or stupid person,

a block-head) praying a stroke
of magic or the next wee drink
turn them from loggerhead
to logodaedalus (cunning in words).

At breakfast, still under the influence,
they're prone to logomachia
(being contentious about words).
And the contentious word holding poets

enthralled through all these centuries
is love, found on page four six three
and refracted over several that follow.
The etymology is a complicated

web of meandaring tributaries:
From OHG gilob: precious
to its Aryan root, Latin's lubet
(libet) pleasing, lubido (libido) desire.

Quickly, then, to the heart of the matter:
Disposition or state of feeling
with regard to a person
which (arising from recognition

of attractive qualities, instinct
of natural relationship or sympathy)
manifests itself in solicitude
for the welfare of the object

and usually delight for his approval.
Theologians, a further entry explains,
distinguish love of complacency
(approval of qualities in the object)

from love of benevolence (bestowed
irrespective of the object's character).
Then, among the proverbs, the sudden insight
that, mercurial as love itself,

There's no love lost between them
meant first one thing, now its exact opposite:
so close were we at one time that in our traffic
there was no love lost between us

but now, in the thick of lawsuits
and at loggerheads (two block-heads
making their lawyers rich)
La! There's no love lost between us.

BEGINNING WITH ISAIAH

I sing to my well-beloved a song,
the song of her making breakfast.
My well-beloved has awakened early
and made ready fire and frying pan.

She brings forth from the cooler
– from the warm nest of our bed
I see with the mind's eye –
choice butter, the eggs of proud hens.

With an ancient wooden spoon
in a chipped blue bowl
held pressed against her breasts
the beloved is stirring, in measures

known only to her – a family secret
whispered down the matrilineal line –
flour, baking soda and buttermilk
seasoned with cinnamon and cloves.

If the first pancake is scorched
this is not an abomination nor a sign
but my beloved tempering the pan
while offering her gods their due.

My beloved must be a magician
for I hear the hiss of coffee rising
her own blend of Arabica,
Harare and Bourbon Santos –

and next, her melodious voice
calling unto me, *awake, Ricardo,*
rise and come into the breakfast nook
and I do so quickly for behold

large, gold, and round as the sun,
that pours light into this room
await three thick pancakes
richly ladled with wild blueberries

picked along the power line
where, yesterday, my beloved met
first a moose and then a bear.
(My well-beloved is fearless.)

We sit in the warm sunlight
and together we break bread.
She offers me coffee and pours.
I am the cup that runneth over.

THE RECKONING

Under the stern tribunal
of his own eyes
(he faces a mirror)
he confesses to everything.

Pointing a finger at himself
(or at his reflection)
he spells out the charges
and the trial begins.

There will be time
for excuses, alibis,
limits to liability
but now the prosecution

is calling its witnesses:
What prodigious memory!
Every long-lost friend
answers the summons

and with such malice,
surely salt has been rubbed
in fading wounds
for grievance to feel this fresh.

With the razor poised
at his lathered throat,
they recite a toxic list
of alleged transgressions

and hint of exhibits to come:
compromising photographs,
inconvenient phone logs.
The case appears irrefutable.

The prosecution rests as he rises
but, presiding judge,
he has dismissed the defence
and makes ready to leave.

The mirror goes dark.
He holds his breath
then plunges his soul
in clean fresh water.

The face in the mirror
gives nothing back as he,
newly shaved, strides out
groomed for further crimes.

THE ALMIGHTY

After Sister gave us Ray-Bans
he dropped the cape and stood
a bristling column of light,
unveiling such mechanisms
as could mend our broken souls:
transgression, remorse, redemption
the circulation of his grace,
the swiftness of his anger.
Be my guest: take my holy name
in vain but first, best consider:
where would you run for cover?
Then he dimmed like a light bulb,
we returned the shades to Sister
and he began a magic trick:

He rummaged through our lunch boxes,
until he found a hard-boiled egg,
blew on it, tucked it in his armpit:
speak to me of resurrections
he said and smiled
and at our silence reached in
to bring out the yellow chick
he set running on Sister's desk.
Behind ours, we sat stunned.

The only sound in the classroom
was the clock and the little chick,
the feathered exegete going chirp,
chirp, pecking at random letters
unscrambling a brand new gospel
from the scribbles of our homework.

IN THE METRO

If only he could
at this late date,
against all odds,
wipe clean the slate

then he might
well convince her
to take him home
and do him right.

If only he could,
but no can do:
lacking now even
the telegraphic grace

of Tarzan-speak,
his half grunts
bear no trace
of what he meant to say

and, nonplussed,
she walks away.
What a headache,
the heart, he thinks:

the way it sleeps
for years only to start
its insidious song
at her sudden apparition.

Knock him down
as he stands there
any child could
with but a feather.

BACK AND FORTH

Of course not, you dope!
Whatever made you think
(*think?* Nothing here but hope!)
love wrote in indelible ink?

Pythagoras had cocked his ears
(or so she mused) and thought
from empty space (no less) he caught
the music of the spheres.

THE BEES

What's with the buzz,
the angry hum I hear
whenever I draw near?

Lovely grump, make nice.
Teach your vengeful bees
the trick (or is it wisdom?)

that allows them to distill
from the thorn of grievance,
the sweetest honey.

ARS LONGA, VITA BREVIS

Sitting upright, at his desk,
primed to begin work right after
this careful twirling of the pencil
round and round the sharpener
being oh so careful not to break
the unfurling wooden banner
he brings up to his nose
to see if it smells of hewn cedar
and it doesn't but just you look
such a lovely strip he managed
to make – but not to measure
since it breaks and by now,
a plastic ruler in his hands,
what exactly he meant to write
has disappeared into the ether
so he goes downstairs and looks
inside the crammed refrigerator
where the carton of milk declares
itself way past its expiry date
which leads to an inspection
of all containers – in such matters
best to be absolutely thorough
and what a mixed haul that yields:
yogurt, cottage cheese and ricotta
but the jar of maraschino cherries
takes the prize, for "best before"

with a date all of five years ago,
in an open can, the tomatoes
are covered with white vellum,
the artichokes are about to expire,
time then to look for the recipe
his brother mailed him
calling for artichoke hearts,
pimento, mushrooms, green
onions and the zest of lemons,
which will afford him another go
at a long, lemon-rind banner
but the soft and wildly sprouting
potatoes should be thrown out
and what about that Idaho senator
looking, they say, for hanky panky
at the airport's bathroom
and surely CNN could by edifying
but this Dalai Lama of procrastination
as he was once called by someone
who knew the discipline it takes
to kill time sees Topples, the cat,
staring unflinchingly at him
who, on the first of her nine lives
has all the time in this world,
and what could a cat ever know
about the state of a man's soul
but perhaps all she means
is my water needs freshening
and as he pours, he notices
the frazzled basil on the sill
could also do with some moisture
but this man should get back to work
and walking up the creaky stairs

he looks at his watch,
sees it is already four-thirty
so best he take a little nap
before his wife comes home,
best, in short, he call it a day.

FISHING

In otherwise beautiful countryside
I found myself at this fishing hole,
a shallow basin below a bridge
where the quick river slowed
to a sluggish, oily, quasi-sludge.
The bridge itself, a poster child
for the nation's decay:
where concrete had flaked off
from the arched underside,
rebars showed a rusty ribcage.
The curve of three or four tires
broke the surface to hold back
a fringe of chemical yellow froth.
Beer cans and pop bottles strewn
over the ground where I stood.
Why ever did I cast? Boredom.
On my way home with no fish,
a few nightcrawlers left in the tin.
No sooner had I flicked my line
dead centre, under the bridge,
I felt the strong tug and struggle
then reeled in a bright, large trout,
sleek and fully jeweled.
That such beauty could emerge
from such a waste of a place
conjured up a spell-bound princess

who, as punishment for misdeeds
or, as often the case, sheer malice
was turned into a fish
forced to live in this dump
until a prince –
I decided to keep the trout
and looked about for a rock
to give it a bop on the head
before laying it in the creel
but my eyes strayed over
the industrial decay of the place,
the toxic whiff of it all
and so, most delicately,
I eased the hook off its lips,
waded into the stream
releasing that quicksilver
right back into the muck.

MORALS

The moral was lost on me
when I was nine and grandfather
read me the fable.
It was the ants that horrified me,
self-righteous clerks
clacking their communal abacus,
bent on blind accumulation,
glutting their hearts on resentment.

A green troubadour with his lute
according to the illustration,
the debonair grasshopper
was what I wished to be.

In bed that night I prayed:
let there have been one ant,
one single ant
that, charmed by song
well into winter
scurried down the corridors
until it reached the gate
where it slipped the hidden crumb
to the dazed, half-dead grasshopper.

And if I can't be the grasshopper,
let me, at the very least, be that ant.

OBIT

She was no Mother Teresa.
You can say that again.
She was no Mother Teresa
and yet, and yet, and yet ...

Something about the way
she gave of herself
generously if temporarily,
just had to remind you

of the gnarled Albanian nun
dispensing tough love
to the riff-raff of Calcutta.
Twinned-purposed, polar opposites:

think Toronto then Tasmania.
Tending, from different ends,
the broken vineyards of the Lord.
So much for her early life.

Back to the comfort of Sion,
she fled the frou-frou of small talk;
marooned in her room
she missed the grit of Babylon.

Here is where I stepped in:
hired to type up from scrawls
the true story of her life.
But her mind meandered

arriving always at sleep
where, as if by dictation,
words I did not know
came to her lips. Was it prayer?

Blissed out in shabby Shangri-La
she hummed along with Doris Day
piped in from the flat below
the fatalism of que será, será.

SKILLS

The melancholy of fulfillment?
Not something he was overly
familiar with though he recalled
when he was eight after months
of rigorous practice he mastered
three nifty moves on the yo-yo
that briefly made him prince
of the playground but since then:

nada

or rather, decades of a dry spell
so when that second marriage hit a reef
and began to take on water
faster than either cared to bail,
he knew precisely the protocols
(here at last was expertise!)
of undoing the binding knots
then deftly captained their pirogue
to the bottom of the sky-blue sea.

How, on those long afternoons,
when my great-aunt Beebee
sat with her sister Tia,
(the two of them knitting)
and stitched together our lives
so that, dispersed, the large clan
gathered in the tent of their words,
did she ever imagine it would end?

And had they dropped a stitch
so part of our story unravelled?
The cousin taken by flames ...
The uncle who disappeared ...

Her son, Haroldo, my mother's cousin,
a man-boy my father's age
(an extra stitch in the chromosomes)
was shaved by Paulito each morning
before sitting down to breakfast
and the exactness of three buttered toasts.
(Changes, however small, undid him.)

Dropped into that household
every afternoon after school
(I was then seven or eight)
today I remember Beebee
setting her knitting aside,
peering over her glasses
as if to gauge the exact
degree of my intractability
then wiping a dry brow,
turn to Tia and say:
Carolina will sweat blood
trying to raise this one.

Later, copying slogans Paulito cooked up
before heading upstairs for his nap,
Haroldo and I practised our penmenship
side by side at the dining room table.

My clumsy scrawl was no match
for his ornate calligraphy
as up and down the page he boasted:
Haroldo é um bom Brasileiro.
Haroldo é um bom Brasileiro.
Haroldo é um bom Brasileiro.

THE WORD

Someone quick!
Fetch this man
a dictionary.

See if he can
on his own
find the name

for what ails him.
Quick to bed
he suffers

sweats, tremors,
sudden jolts
that awake him:

an icy finger
slowly tracing
a bent spine.

No word he knows
can name this funk
though he swears

when found such word
(to name is to tame)
will prove a balm

that quiets the heart,
allows it sleep.
Here. Start with the A's.

She came in with the grocery bag
in the crook of her left arm,
eased it on the kitchen counter
and ran to the bathroom, calling
out to let him know she was home
but heard him in the basement or
rather, heard the whine of his saw.
She washed her hands, touched up her hair,
and walked back into the kitchen
to stand by the sink looking out
at a precocious poplar
that began to change its colours
though here it was but September
and such a bright, gorgeous yellow.
She reached for the phone on the wall
thinking she should speak to Betty
but then, thought better of it,
reached instead for a Kleenex.
The whine of the saw stopped.
She walked to the basement door
opened it and called down "Hi Jeff
I'm home, honey" and heard him
call back "hi, sweetie, up in a jiffy."
Jeff would be up in a jiffy
she thought in sing-song
then of the roast she'd bought

and of what else to serve alongside,
wondering whether she had garlic
in case she went with green beans
then reaching into the grocery bag
brought out the bottle of Chianti
and thought wild-rice, green beans,
stir-fried mushrooms would nicely do
as she poured what she herself called
"a generous glass" but remembered,
before sitting down, to transfer
the clothes from washer to dryer.
She liked the smell of laundry soap
and of wet laundry itself,
the tangle of their clothes.
The noise they made, tumbling,
was soothing as she sipped her wine.
Let sleeping dogs lie, she thought
and whispered we'll do fine, just fine.

Truth be told,
I wish she would
unkiss me,

turn me back
into the frog I was
and happy being.

Give me back nights
I dared the moon,
fat and round,

to step down
and skinny dip
until dawn.

My velvet britches?
This silver crown?
Nothing here even close

to those moments
when she dropped her cloak,
tested the waters

with her toes
then slipped in and silvered
my dark pond.

BIOGRAPHY

So far as he could tell
no playbook, script or set
of directions: things happened
to happen, others followed
willy-nilly and he went along
for what he thought of as the ride.

Less a life than narrative flow
with its demand to keep on
going, keeping on, that is,
until that final cul-de-sac
where, abruptly the story ends
before all the narrative strands,
the plots that led to this plot
were gathered together in a whole.

BERKELEY IS IN BRAZIL

At ninety-three his inner world prevails,
obliterates what the senses could tell him
as to his real location were he to just look
out of his windows: a house perched
in the Berkeley hills, overlooking the Bay;
a toy bridge, the Golden Gate shimmers
through fog and rain, far away.

None of this proves ballast enough. No.
He is in Brazil. In Petrópolis again.
But thinking of driving down to Rio.
Tomorrow. If it stops raining.

Or: at home, he thinks he's in the hospital
where, mysteriously, the paintings he owns
by Frank, his childhood friend, also hang.

We ache at the effort he makes
to make sense of this confusion:
the hospital ... the home ... Frank's paintings ...
Until he finally squares the circle:

The house is in the hospital!
The university offered some professors
the chance to buy these hospital-homes.
Although he can't remember signing papers
he has two homes: the one in Berkeley
and this one at Kaiser-Oakland.

"Your mother had both houses painted
exactly the same: I get confused!"

KINGS

King of Catarrh,
my next-door neighbour,
hails the morning sun
doing what he does best:
coughing up dead music.

This steady hack,
and chain of whoops
are his attempts to drain
the bog that is his chest.

Once begun, the tractor
works a good two hours
clearing muck from roads
that, branching, reach
every clogged alveoli;
soundtrack to breakfast
on my side of the wall
or, today, as it happens,
to this chess game
where Luciano, I note,
left his flank exposed
bent on a clever attack
all flair but sure to fail.

I move a sly and lowly pawn.

There! With that harrumph
the King tractors through
some final blockage
and into his lungs flow
oxygen that is then exhaled
as song: his croak of longing
for the sun-drenched island
they all call home.

And now, my turn to gasp.
Lu himself moves a pawn
uncovering Episcopal mischief:
his black Bishop in cahoots
with the sashaying queen.
Checkmate in two moves.

MANUAL

One way to do it:
occupy the white beach
of the page with words:
(supply interminable)
lay siege, then breech
by sheer volume
and manic insistence
the intransigence of silence.
Try to wrest
from the ensuing din,
some garbled message,
then take that home
and mull it over:
i.e. revise, revise.

Or, another tack:
grown abstemious,
to hoard the words
or dispense them
homeopathically
slowly, one by one,
watching the circles
each makes as it breaks
the surface of the paper
divining in the design
some hermetic message,
a truce freshly signed,
between word and world
and having registered it
consider the job done.

Knowing it is never done,
a provisional victory at best
that no sooner inked
proves ephemeral, obsolete,
insufficient,
the world (or is it us?)
refusing to stand still
so that what little clarity
is achieved quickly dims
as the word engine starts
again at the very start:
to stutter its way towards truth
or lies and be, at the end,
unable to tell them apart.

SOME DANCE

A little sauced,
you claim to hear
the music of the spheres
and when you say

some stars are stars
that ring slightly off
as if the grand tuner
had grown distracted

or preoccupied or drank
too much at lunch time
and lost his perfect pitch
I'm ready to agree.

This loss of pitch
is what you claim
makes the universe amenable.
By that small discord

it becomes more human,
as if that mistake
if mistake it was
brought *us* in tune:

we and the universe
and after a dinner
where we drank
a bit too much,

standing side by side,
we do the dishes.
I notice the constellation
tattooed on your shoulders,

how the stars ripple
as if refracted under water.
You wash and rinse,
I dry and stack

and then you turn off
the kitchen light and ask
would you like to dance
and when I ask when

you say now and then
turn to turn the radio on,
the music begins
and we begin to dance.

ACKNOWLEDGMENTS

Earlier versions of some of these poems appeared in *The Walrus, Descant, The Literary Review of Canada, Maisonneuve, Exile, Poesis,* and *The Fiddlehead.*

"New Canaan," initially published in *The Literary Review Canada,* was chosen for the *Best Canadian Poetry* anthology, 2009, edited by A.F. Moritz.

"Blues," initially published in *The Fiddlehead,* was chosen for the *Best Canadian Poetry* anthology, 2012, edited by Carmine Starnino.

For help with these poems over the years I am grateful to my wife, Christine McCormick Sternberg, and to many friends including Clive Holden, Molly Peacock, Richard Sanger, Doug Thompson, and Alissa York. I am especially grateful to Sheila Dwight for her patient and thoughtful comments on early drafts of practically all these poems. The poem "Manual" is dedicated to her.